fun to color and do

I Wonder What Jesus Would Do?
Activities

By
Laura Wasson Warfel

Cover Illustration by
Dan Sharp

Inside Illustrations by
Anthony Carpenter

Publisher
In Celebration™
a division of Instructional Fair Group
Grand Rapids, Michigan 49544

Permission to Reproduce

About the Book

Each of the activities in this book encourages young children to think about the question "What would Jesus do?" Children will enjoy the variety of fun activities presented. You the parent/teacher will appreciate the opportunity to guide children toward the goal of growing more like Jesus through the activities, memory verses, and scripture references found on each page.

Credits

Author: Laura Wasson Warfel
Cover Artist: Dan Sharp
Inside Illustrations: Anthony Carpenter
Project Director/Editor: Alyson Kieda
Editors: Linda Triemstra,
        Meredith Van Zomeren
Graphic Layout: Deborah Hanson McNiff

About the Author

Laura Wasson Warfel enjoys telling children about Jesus. God gives her many opportunities to do so. She is a Christian education teacher, a stepmom to two sons and a daughter, and a minister's wife. A professional writer and workshop presenter, she lives in Guthrie, Oklahoma, where you can find her petting her cats or playing with her dog on just about any day.

Standard Book Number: 0-7424-0020-4
I Wonder What Jesus Would Do? . . . Activities
Copyright © 2000 by In Celebration™
a division of Instructional Fair Group
a Tribune Education Company
3195 Wilson Dr. NW
Grand Rapids, Michigan 49544

— W.W.J.D? —
He would help others.

Scripture Verse: "The good man brings good things out of the good stored up in his heart" (Luke 6:45).

How can we help others? Color inside the solid black lines to discover some ways.

Scripture Reference: A Tree's Fruit (Luke 6:43–45)

— W.W.J.D? —
He would care for the sick.

Scripture Verse: "Be kind and compassionate to one another" (Ephesians 4:32a).

What are some things you can do to be kind to someone who is sick? Find these words in the puzzle: *talk, food, help, games, quiet, pray, love, read, draw, drink, share, care.*

```
S S I A R T A L K T
E H T R N S E N D N
N A R I S D F O O D
E R G A M E S H A S
R E D R I N K H C R
N E E E R D R R P S
H E L P A N T T U W
B L E N T O N L D R
N O Q U I E T A R E
E V F T C A R E A A
M E Y S P R A Y W D
```

Scripture Reference: The Sick Healed (Matthew 4:23–25)

— W.W.J.D? —
He would share with others.

Scripture Verse: "When you give to the needy, do not let your left hand know what your right hand is doing, so that your giving may be in secret" (Matthew 6:3–4).

Sometimes it's easy to tell what others need. Draw a line from each person to what he or she needs.

Scripture Reference: Giving to Those in Need (Matthew 6:1–4)

— W.W.J.D? —
He would talk to God.

Scripture Verse: "The LORD has heard my cry for mercy; the LORD accepts my prayer" (Psalm 6:9).

Can you find the letters that spell *prayer* in this picture?

Scripture References: Prayer (Matthew 6:5–15); Jesus Prays (Mark 1:35); Gethsemane (Matthew 26:36–45)

—— W.W.J.D? ——
He would ask God for what he needs.

Scripture Verse: "I pray to you, O Lᴏʀᴅ; . . . in your great love, O God, answer me" (Psalm 69:13).

What are some things that you can talk to God about? Find these words in the puzzle: *school, family, fear, joy, friends, food, love, pets, worry, sins.*

```
J O Y E S C H O O L
E S U A I V M M U I
C E R A T L G I E I
E F F F R I E N D S
E E T L O V E N T F
E A Q P W H A S O A
T R R T I D T I D M
X V B I F C I N S I
U W O R R Y O S S L
W A R F O O D P V Y
S D L H I T E H O P
S Y S O I P E T S T
```

Scripture Reference: Ask, Seek, Knock (Matthew 7:7–12)

— W.W.J.D? —
He would build his life on God.

Scripture Verse: "The LORD is my rock, my fortress and my deliverer" (Psalm 18:2a).

A rebus tells the story of the wise and foolish builders.

There once was a wise [man]. He wanted to build a [house]. He looked for a good place. Then he saw a [rock]. He said, "This is where I will [hammer/build] my [house]."

Not far from the wise [man] lived another [man] who wasn't very smart. He wanted to build a [house]. He looked for a place. Then he saw a pile of [sand]. He said, "This is where I will [hammer/build] my [house]."

The [rain] came down. The [water] came up. The [wind] blew.

Which [house] was still standing when the storm stopped? The [house] on the [rock] stood tall. The [house] on the [sand] lay flat.

Jesus is our [rock]. When we trust and obey him, we will stand tall.

Scripture Reference: The Wise and Foolish Builders (Matthew 7:24–27)

He would follow God, no matter what.

Scripture Verse: "Follow [Jesus] wherever he goes" (Revelation 14:4).

Can you get to Jesus? Find your way along the path.

Scripture References: The Cost of Following Jesus (Matthew 8:18–22); A Prophet Without Honor (Mark 6:1–6); Jesus Rejected (Luke 4:14–30)

W.W.J.D?
He would trust God to help him.

Scripture Verse: "Trust in the LORD with all your heart and lean not on your own understanding" (Proverbs 3:5).

Connect the dots to find out who stopped the storm.

Scripture Reference: Jesus Calms the Storm (Matthew 8:23–27)

— W.W.J.D? —
He would reach out to others.

Scripture Verse: "Keep on loving each other as brothers" (Hebrews 13:1).

What is different about these pictures?

Scripture Reference: Jesus Calls Matthew (Matthew 9:9–13)

W.W.J.D?
He would tell others about God.

Scripture Verse: "What I tell you in the dark, speak in the daylight; what is whispered in your ear, proclaim from the roofs" (Matthew 10:27).

We go to church and read the Bible to learn about God. Write a story about how you could tell someone else about God. Draw a picture to illustrate your story.

Scripture Reference: Jesus Sends Out the Disciples (Matthew 10)

W.W.J.D?
He would trust God for all that he needs.

Scripture Verse: "And my God will meet all your needs according to his glorious riches in Christ Jesus" (Philippians 4:19).

Make the bottom picture look like the top picture. Draw what is missing.

Scripture References: Jesus Feeds 5,000 (Matthew 14:13–21); Jesus Feeds 4,000 (Matthew 15:29–39)

He would choose God over everything else.

Scripture Verse: Jesus said, "Whoever follows me will never walk in darkness, but will have the light of life" (John 8:12).

Use the Secret Code to fill in the letters. Find out the choice Jesus wants you to make.

Message:

$\overline{10}\ \overline{11}\ \overline{13}\ \overline{13}\ \overline{11}\ \overline{6}$ $\overline{9}\ \overline{12}\ \overline{2}\ \overline{15}\ \overline{2}$ $\overline{3}\ \overline{1}\ \overline{5}$

$\overline{6}\ \overline{3}\ \overline{13}\ \overline{7}$ $\overline{16}\ \overline{1}$ $\overline{14}\ \overline{8}\ \overline{12}$ $\overline{13}\ \overline{16}\ \overline{4}\ \overline{8}\ \overline{14}$.

Secret Code:

3 = A	7 = K
5 = D	13 = L
12 = E	1 = N
10 = F	11 = O
4 = G	2 = S
8 = H	14 = T
16 = I	15 = U
9 = J	6 = W

Scripture Reference: At Mary and Martha's Home (Luke 10:38–42)

— W.W.J.D? —
He would care for those with troubles.

Scripture Verse: "Let us not love with words . . . but with actions" (1 John 3:18).

How can we show others we care for them? Circle the pictures that fit. Put an X through those that don't.

Scripture Reference: The Good Samaritan (Luke 10:25–37).

— **W.W.J.D?**

He would trust God to take care of him.

Scripture Verse: Jesus said, "Do not let your hearts be troubled. Trust in God; trust also in me" (John 14:1).

Make up a story to go with each picture.

Scripture Reference: Do Not Worry (Luke 12:22–34)

— W.W.J.D? —
He would welcome everyone to God's house.

Scripture Verse: "The same Lord is Lord of all and richly blesses all who call on him, for, 'Everyone who calls on the name of the Lord will be saved'" (Romans 10:12–13).

Who does God want to see in church with you? Finish this picture.

Scripture Reference: Jesus at a Pharisee's House (Luke 14:1–24)

— W.W.J.D? —
He would let God work through him.

Scripture Verse: Jesus said, "As long as it is day, we must do the work of him who sent me" (John 9:4).

Unscramble these words to find out some of the ways that God wants us to work for him.

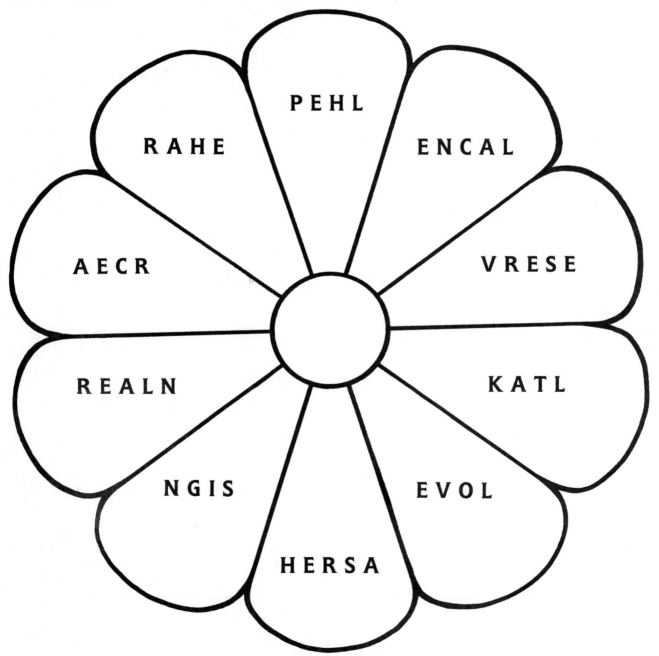

Scripture Reference: Jesus Walks on Water (Matthew 14:22–36)

IF9927 I Wonder What Jesus Would Do? . . . Activities

— W.W.J.D? —
He would help others find their way to God.

Scripture Verse: Jesus said, "Your Father in heaven is not willing that any . . . should be lost" (Matthew 18:14).

Wind your way through the maze to help the shepherd find his sheep.

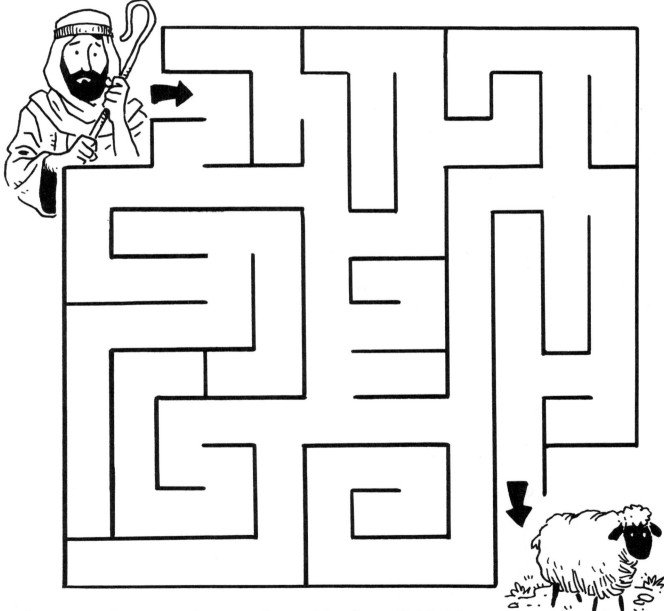

Scripture Reference: The Lost Sheep (Matthew 18:10–14)

— W.W.J.D? —
He would forgive
others when they hurt him.

Scripture Verse: "Forgive your brother from your heart" (Matthew 18:35).

Color the spaces that have dots to discover the secret word.

Scripture References: The Unmerciful Servant (Matthew 18:21–35); Peter Denies Christ (John 18:15–18, 25–27); Jesus Reinstates Peter (John 21:15–25)

— W.W.J.D? —
He would give up
everything he had to serve God.

Scripture Verse: "Jesus said to Simon, . . . 'From now on you will catch men.' So they . . . left everything and followed [Jesus]" (Luke 5:10–11).

Peter had to give up his fishing net to follow Jesus. Draw a line to connect the person(s) to the thing they might have to give up to follow Jesus.

Scripture Reference: The Rich Young Man (Matthew 19:16–30)

— W.W.J.D? —
He would love and comfort those who are sad.

Scripture Verse: "As a mother comforts her child, so will I comfort you" (Isaiah 66:13).

Jesus is always with you. Draw who's missing in each picture.

Scripture Reference: Jesus Comforts Mary and Martha (John 11:17–37)

IF9927 I Wonder What Jesus Would Do? . . . Activities

— W.W.J.D? —
He would obey God.

Scripture Verse: "Jesus replied, 'If anyone loves me, he will obey my teaching'" (John 14:23).

What does Jesus want us to do? Find two words in this picture that tell you.

Scripture Reference: The Two Sons (Matthew 21:28–32)

— W.W.J.D? —
He would show God's love
by what he did.

Scripture Verse: "I will show you my faith by what I do" (James 2:18b).

Find these words in the picture and color them: *show, faith, love, do, others.* Then color the rest of the picture.

Scripture Reference: Jesus Anointed (Mark 14:1–11)

— W.W.J.D? —
He would love God, himself, and everyone.

Scripture Verse: "Love the Lord your God with all your heart and with all your soul and with all your mind and with all your strength. . . . Love your neighbor as yourself" (Mark 12:30–31).

Fill in the missing letters. Then match the picture with the word.

LO _ E   G _ _

_ OVE   M _

L _ V _   MO _   AND   D _ D

L _ VE   JE _ _ S

_ O _ E   F _ IEND _

_ _ VE   SI _ TE _   AND   BR _ THE _

Scripture Reference: The Greatest Commandment (Mark 12:28–34)

— W.W.J.D? —
He would serve and care for others.

Scripture Verse: "Be devoted to one another. . . . Honor one another above yourselves" (Romans 12:10).

Draw a line from each picture on the left to the picture on the right that matches.

Scripture Reference: Jesus Washes the Disciples' Feet (John 13:1–17)

— W.W.J.D? —
He would trust in God's plan.

Scripture Verse: "The plans of the LORD stand firm forever" (Psalm 33:11).

Use the Secret Code to fill in the letters. Find out the choice Jesus wants you to make.

Message:

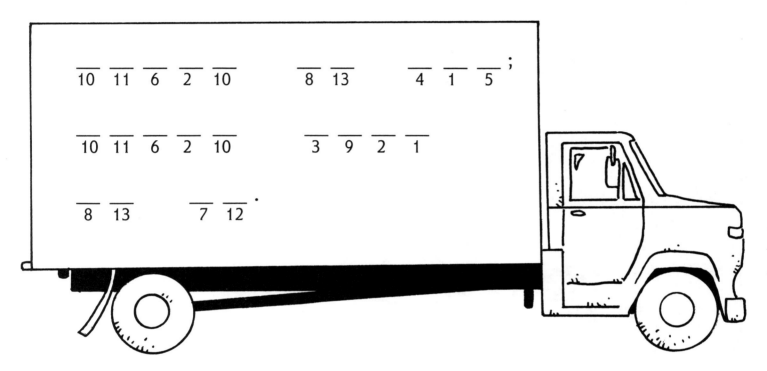

$$\overline{10}\ \overline{11}\ \overline{6}\ \overline{2}\ \overline{10}\qquad \overline{8}\ \overline{13}\qquad \overline{4}\ \overline{1}\ \overline{5}\ ;$$

$$\overline{10}\ \overline{11}\ \overline{6}\ \overline{2}\ \overline{10}\qquad \overline{3}\ \overline{9}\ \overline{2}\ \overline{1}$$

$$\overline{8}\ \overline{13}\qquad \overline{7}\ \overline{12}\ .$$

Secret Code:

3 = A	13 = N
5 = D	1 = O
12 = E	11 = R
4 = G	2 = S
8 = I	10 = T
9 = L	6 = U
7 = M	

Scripture Reference: Jesus Comforts Disciples (John 14:1–4)

— W.W.J.D? —
He would obey God's commands.

Scripture Verse: Jesus said, "Remain in me, and I will remain in you. . . . Showing yourselves to be my disciples" (John 15:4, 8).

Color the picture by numbers: 1 = green   2 = black   3 = brown   4 = blue   5 = yellow

Scripture Reference: Vine and Branches (John 15:1–17)

— W.W.J.D? —
He would do what God calls him to do.

Scripture Verse: "As for God, his way is perfect; the word of the LORD is flawless" (2 Samuel 22:31).

Connect the dots to find out what Jesus did for us.

Scripture Reference: The Crucifixion (Matthew 27:32–44)

— W.W.J.D? —
He would tell us
how to be saved from our sin.

Scripture Verse: Jesus said, "Whoever lives and believes in me will never die" (John 11:26).

What is different in these pictures?

Scripture Reference: Jesus' Resurrection (Matthew 28:1–10)

— W.W.J.D? —
He would tell others about God's love and how God has saved us from our sin.

Scripture Verse: "God [shows] his . . . love for us in this: While we were still sinners, Christ died for us" (Romans 5:8).

Make up a story to go with this picture.

Scripture Reference: The Great Commission (Matthew 28:16–20)

Answer Key

Page 4

Page 7

Page 14
FOLLOW JESUS AND
WALK IN THE LIGHT.

Page 18
HELP
CLEAN
SERVE
TALK
LOVE
SHARE
SING
LEARN
CARE
HEAR

Page 25
LOVE GOD
LOVE ME
LOVE MOM AND DAD
LOVE JESUS
LOVE FRIENDS
LOVE SISTER AND BROTHER

Page 27
TRUST IN GOD;
TRUST ALSO IN ME.